VIA FOLIOS 97

D1715206

The Mandate of Heaven

Select Poems

Grace Cavalieri

BORDIGHERA PRESS

Library of Congress Control Number: 2014941913

COVER PHOTO: Dan Murano

© 2014 by Grace Cavalieri

All rights reserved. Parts of this book may be reprinted only by written permission from the author, and may not be reproduced for publication in book, magazine, or electronic media of any kind, except for purposes of literary reviews by critics.

Printed in the United States.

Published by
BORDIGHERA PRESS
John D. Calandra Italian American Institute
25 West 43rd Street, 17th Floor
New York, NY 10036

VIA FOLIOS 97
ISBN 978-1-59954-075-7

Grateful Acknowledgements for poems reprinted:

Sit Down Says Love (Argonne House Press)
Swan Research (The Word Works)
Sounds Like Something I Would Say (Casa Menendez Publishers)
Trenton (Belle Mead Press)
Migrations (Vision Library)
Water on the Sun (Bordighera Press)

Charles Olson.

THESE DAYS
whatever you have to say, leave
the roots on, let them
dangle

And the dirt

Just to make clear
where they come from

TABLE OF CONTENTS

Letters	1
Ancestors	3
Nettie and Angelo	5
Birth	8
Father	10
Ellsworth Avenue	12
Carciofi (Artichokes)	14
The Mandate of Heaven	16
The Secret Jew	18
The First	20
Dates	22
Time Travel	24
Grandmother	27
Tomato Pies, 25 Cents	29
Senior Prom	31
Trenton Transit	33
Angelo	35
Stage Makeup	36
Moderation	38
Nettie	40
Judy and Me	43
Summer in the Convent	46
To His House	46
Replacing Loss	48
Things That Hurried By	50
Markings	53
This Is	55

You Could Not Say
     She Was Of This Earth   56

Meeting of The Heavenly Ancestors   57

Place of Listening   58

The Magician   59

In Search of My Grandfather
     Three Sestinas   61

Expression   66

Blue Green Spirit   68

ABOUT THE AUTHOR   71

The Mandate of Heaven

LETTERS

If you ask what brings us here,
staring out of our lives

like animals in high grass,
I'd say it was what we had in common

with the other—the hum of a song we
believe in which can't be heard,

the sound of our own
luminous bodies rising just behind the hill,

the dream of a light which won't go out,
and a story we're never finished with.

We talk of things we cannot comprehend
so that you'll know about

the inner and the outer world which are the same.
Someone has to be with us in this,

and if you are, then,
you know us best. And I mean all of us,

the deer who leaves his marks behind him
in the snow, the red fox moving through the woods.

The same stream in them is in us too
although we are the chosen ones who speak.

Please tell me what you think cannot be sold
and I will say that's all there is:

the pain in our lives
...the thoughts we have...

We bring these small seeds.
Do what you can with them.

What is found in this beleaguered
and beautiful land is what we write of.

ANCESTORS

I have followed the slow vine
   from where they came –
that country with olive trees
   and more – to find it not
that different from my own.
   In each place the grandfather
was born to fail or so
   he thought. The grandmother
held it well, making
   small briquettes to keep a fire.

In my own house we thought
   it didn't matter, those who went
before, but that was not true. We'll never
   get warm enough without
the dung from all the animals in
   our past lost on the hill. We stack
it in a corner, call it fuel and
   start again their fire. Floating in
the space between are all
   my children. Here's the one

who took charge of others
   when they fell in mud and needed
a clean dress. There is
   the one who wanted to be alone.
Next to her the twin who wanted
   her own sister. And later another

3

sitting outside the hallway
   for thirty minutes every day so I could
write. They would describe the
   space they float in differently. They

would say they wanted all
   they got and all they needed.
I stand outside and wish
   to enter but cannot. It is their
property, I have my own.

Between us are the years
   stacked like dishes,
one upon the other, some clean,
   some with the grime of
regret. We abandon our children

when they are birthed
   because we breathe
them into separate light.
   A passage isn't there for me
although my face is on their bodies.

Build the fire that you can:
   Raphael, Giudita, Graziela, Philip,
Nettie, Angelo, Grace, and Ken,
   Cynthia, Colleen, Shelley, Angela,
over the narrow bridge to the animals.

NETTIE AND ANGELO

She didn't know what marriage
  could possibly mean

or what would happen to her.
  Her mother only said

he was the right one and the
  gown would have a train, white satin

that dripped down seven steps.
  Nettie didn't know Angelo

except by the food he ordered in the family
  restaurant. He always

sat at the first table. She
  always worked the register.

Her parents made his pasta
  fresh for him, everytime, their favorite

customer, the one who would marry their
  daughter. How could she

want something she didn't know?
  How could she know

someone she didn't want?
  Her sister Rose would chaperone,

would go on all their dates and
   that bridesmaid, Rose,

wore the only satin gown
   she'd ever wear.

Lucky Rose—only to care for
   children at Easter and Christmas

while my mother
   who couldn't find what food to cook

or how to dry wet snowsuits
   every day would somehow set our table.

Rosie took over at the register
   while customers would come and go,

but Nettie stayed quiet,
   and drifted from our kitchen

until the beautiful Nettie couldn't remember
   how to count the change.

Chastity, obedience, silence, poverty
   broken pieces coming together

to build the house in the sky.
   When you know the heart and look into

its strange surprise
   why can't we describe it,

or find the evidence for what
   was real, or say what was

illusion, or see whatever pulls the soul
   from the body to live outside itself.

BIRTH

From the smoke lying like an umbrella
over the fields
from the line of pine trees along the road
from the acorn shaped trees of Italy
from the light on the hill.

a child is born.

You can feel it...
You can see it...

Before loosening up into the air
a house is growing for her

Before a house will be boarded up
it is opening for her

The child will never be more
than she was

She will never be less
than in other times

She will be in a different place
from anything ever loved before

Lucky she does not know
what is waiting on the other side

how the earth needs
her protection

how she is to find
something to believe in

Birth was not the gift she wanted

but if it does not go away
in time
like an illness or an ache

she will find
light off the river
enough to see by

and some good to say of it

She will find attachment, amazement
She will be free
to surround herself with her own life.

FATHER

When I see the 1900's walk by
          in early frock coat from a former time
I see you in grey and brown like
          New York, its cold cement,
Small canisters of milk carried
          downstairs by children
Who could not speak the language;
          I hear the chicken freezing
In your yard, let loose so
          you could eat that night.
And of the pack of you,
          squabbling and squawking in the corner
No regard is given by your
          Queen Mother sitting in the
Chair, embroidering her dream of
          Florence where there were
Stables, the town apartment in
          Venice, the fields to the
North around Pisa, sewing the colors she knew
          on fine silk.

When I think of your father, the professor
          coming home, without money, paid once more
In love and adulation by the crowds,
          in their dialect
And how he died with pennies on his eyelids,
          the secret note speaking
Of his failures to you, my father, the eldest,
          did you know

Where to go with that pain? How ashamed
        you must be of us;
Your brother's sons are physicians, physicists
        researching the stars
And he, eighteen months younger than you,
        spared again.

ELLSWORTH AVENUE

It started with a bad taste in the mouth

This language parting the tongue;

Where was there to go but to the attic

Windows reaching trees

Talking, always talking to the

Mirrors, in my satin shoes and colored stones.

Talking to the pages in the fake white drawers

Because you wouldn't listen:

Muriel, with your Quaker parents, floating by,

Speaking silver tones made into napkin rings,

Elaine, not allowed animals or friends inside

Because your father still sees his prisoners die,

Jean, and mother, the comedian

Pretending her arm pulled your head from the door,

Mr. Sprague, on a porch above the hardware store,

Mrs. Levine, because you couldn't speak English

And your son gassed himself

In his dentist chair,

Mrs. Milacci, although one daughter was crazy

And I made the other one cry

                              didn't you know

I would have carried roses through the snow?

I would bring you a cake on Sunday.

CARCIOFI (artichokes)

For Rafael Cavalieri

One by one things fall away,
everything but the sweet earth itself.
Already this year he has watched the nest's
careful brush of twigs lose a summer song.

He leans his bicycle against the tree. Tuscany
never changes, they say, but the mountains
seem small, each season, as he goes north

toward Pietrasanta. Only carciofi remain the same, clustered
to the earth. Year after year, this time, the tough fruit
is left for the last of those who want it.

My grandfather picks them here, although he
is not a farmer, he knows where on the stem
to reach. A scholar who saw the world as
a work of art, he holds them like this,

carries them back to his small apartment
past the piazza, behind the university wall.
Pisa. Can you see the dirt on his hands, as he
cups them close, their hard skins,
dusty particles beneath his nails.

What moved him to hunger, and when, that night
we can't know, but that he ate carciofi, the diary
reveals; a plant flavored with olive oil.
Maybe after the lamp was lit, a tiny flask

of oil was brought out, pressings
from a vat near Granoia, adding
salt from a bowl, the mineral
makes a fragrance rise, enough to move him to
open the small window and, by luck, hear a nightingale.

Later he will lean over his drawings. But right now he
puts the finished leaves in a bowl. This is the man who
imagined the gas-driven tractor which would
someday ride the fields of uneven ground.

Tonight there is only the vision of a vehicle
in his head, for he feels refreshed after dining.
How strange to rest, brushing his hand across the
linen, smudging it, without thought.
il paese della meraviglia. He will
visit the farmer again, take from his fields,

But for now the mind feasts on what the eye has
seen, villas with ochre walls, pink terra cotta roofs,
factories with old doors, the ride out of town
pedaling past olive groves, apple trees pinned against

fences, pruned grape vines ready to burst,
covers pulled taut over seeded ground, the sun traveling
to the sea, peaceful snow on the mountains.
Everywhere he looks, the land ready for a new way to harvest.

THE MANDATE OF HEAVEN

I'm not sure where it began
in the dozens of stories in the books of wisdom
or the story behind the story
but the power in the writing wants to be released
during this one lifetime—
Not much to go on, with the fears, guilt and rage,
but through these lay the inner path
to the eternal and the unending
story which will be moved somehow through me,
my ancestors, if you
will tell me who you are and bless what I do.

If we could finish the unfinished
what would we say, what themes would we play today,
what violence, death, abandonment and loss would
we see—how would I seek the inner harmony
which you speak of, but have left undone.

The inner mystery,
the memory of you, I thank you—
Gratitude is one miracle you
teach in the long story you sang and wrote, saying of life
"the only way out is all the way through"
and since you have done that before me
you build a long bridge of high truth for me to cross

carrying the story, the mutable story,
the one that has a habit of happening again and again

with its unforgiving music and forgiving spirits—
This time the words you hummed in each other's ears at night
and at work, reside here in my body with all their unfinished
feelings, breathing for my life.

THE SECRET JEW

Grandfather,
among the Italians, you were a scholar and a Jew —
how is it we were never told your secret life
at Pisa, a PhD before your time, secret wealth,
lumber in Trieste —

only an uncle to raise you,
this must be why a woman caught your eye and
hunger overcame you.
When your moon was lighted by the sun of a
Catholic, your family said Kaddish for their loss,

you came to America, penniless
with a blue-eyed wife and seven children to find
this county wanted nothing from you —
a literary man who couldn't even build a subway —
Why'd You Come? they asked,

but what matters more is your son, my father, who
thought your disinheritance a family shame and never
spoke your name as Jew, so we never knew, thinking
you an old Italian who couldn't use his hands.

Finding out now who you were
I dedicate this poem to you, old Jew,
who gave up land for love.
They say everyone writes for one person,
I will write for you.

No more ecstasies for me and visionary dreams of
    sleep,
I will THINK my way toward death—
then wild with centuries of success, I will argue with
    God
and interpret my way into Heaven with the best of
    them,

I hope to find you, old man, with the riches of Italy you
left behind, with my father
at your side, and Giudita, your bride
doing what all Jews do,
resting from their wanderings
reading from their ancient books,
dear silent grandfather, united with your sons
now among the proudest ones.

Nothing of you remains but my song which begins:
"My fellow Jews! I am of Rafael Cavalieri! And before
    him
other great people, probably smart people, rich people,
rabbis, and lawyers and scholars no doubt—I find I am
    with
you—suddenly a Jew!"

THE FIRST

Mrs. Conti was the first
blonde Italian I ever knew
she didn't have any children
she was the first
who had a husband
with a mistress
Mr. Conti was the first man
with money enough
to have a mistress
whiskey money
he bootlegged whiskey once
and now, a czar in Trenton
his wife could drive a car
Mrs. Conti was
the first one of our friends
with free time and her own car
she'd visit our house on Thursdays
"Poor Veronica"
my parents would say—poor Veronica
she had purses of every color and size
purses were no problem for Mrs. Conti
she gave me all the old ones
smelling of tobacco and perfume
Veronica was the only woman
I'd ever seen
smoke a cigarette
at least in those days
except in the movies

the black patent leather purse
was my favorite
a gold satin lining
shiny and fine
kept in tissue by my paper dolls
filling the room with a mysterious scent
once I put my Sonja Henie doll inside
she came out covered with smoke
adultery, sadness
and lust
beautiful Sonja
her strong muscles
her upraised arms
her tiny sparkling skirts
smooth legs
strong knees
a skater who could cut figures with the angels
a natural blonde
clean and able
a champion
she could drive a car anywhere she wanted
she didn't have to fill her time on Thursdays.

DATES

The silver from my mother's mirror
gleams its stories
toward a light which drops and never breaks.
It says to tell the truth and

permanently shining, brings forth
an original day bright as this one
where children and other small creatures
played without threat

but the child's story is never without fear—is it—
and seems to be made of remainders which either
want for love or some relief of it.

In the third grade the pyramids were presented to us
by Miss O'Malley,
so kind that she would—
in honor of learning—
give us the key to Egypt
if she could.
Who would like to bring in dates for all to taste?
Who can do this on the lunch hour? she asked,
Naturally I
—who could not imagine how—
said I would—
and, like a child with enough money to spend, ran
home
with only one hour, one hour to ease

my dear mother who probably had
little money in the house, yet who bravely asked
"Shouldn't you by *two* packages for the class"
I said No.
Love and fear divided in my mind between
an ocean of children
and my mother's troubled face,

"One package is all I need!" I lied,
"Someone else will bring the rest"
(children spend so much time persuading—
no wonder no one believes them).
Eight dates for twenty children
which would taste so sweet—
Miss O'Malley, always kind, cut the tiny squares
and I kept interrupting, hoping they
wouldn't notice. After all
there wasn't water in the land of pyramids . . . was
there . . . and
not too many trees
probably hungry people and small rations there as
well.

That day every one of us was a reflection of the other—
the children who ate their portions,
the mother at home worrying about her daughter's gift,
the child thinking about her mother's face
and Miss O'Malley who, kind and earnest,
taught us all about a hardy people in an arid land
who gave what they had and could give nothing more.

TIME TRAVEL

My father was the brightest, most promising

young man at the bank,

or so he was told – smart, articulate

good with numbers, kind to the

customers, drawing in Italians from

the neighborhood. He read their

letters from the Old Country, planned

savings so their sons could go to college.

He was the best there was, that must

be why the President called him in

his large office, offering an unexpected

prize – to be an officer

of The Banking Company. How

good my father must have felt. Was he

flushed with surprise? excited?

"However," the head man

said, "you'll have to change

your last name. You understand. A bank

officer is different from an ordinary teller."

What was his first thought? What scene did he

see? His own father, Rafael, in Pisa,

at the University? The young agronomist

leaning over his drawings of a

gas-driven tractor designed to harvest

the vineyards? What did he remember

of the Piazza dei Cavalieri – or of the

company which took the patent away without

credit or cash, or Rafael in this new country,

with a final note to his children of his failures.

How many moments did it take

Before my father refused the

offer? Did he look at the clock on

the wall, move his feet on the

carpet, turning slowly to the door?

Twenty years later, he

obtained the desk after all,

nearly one hundred years away

from his father,

Pisa, & California, harvesting

its grapes with the gas-driven

engine, common machinery, now. All things

moving slowly, just a matter of time.

GRANDMOTHER

for Graziela Zoda

What is the purpose of visits to me twice since you've
    died?

Downstairs near a woodstove I hear you
in motion, always working,
a long silken dress—
tight sleeves at your wrist, soft above the elbow
wide top at your shoulder for free movement.

When we were young you didn't visit—
you never baked a cake that I remember
or babysat or held me in your lap.
you were in the men's part of town running a man's
    business
calling the world to order,
seven children behind you
raised singlehandedly in your large house. You were
moving, always moving.

When I kept losing things like my parents,
    my children, money
my time and health
why did you appear in my room with gifts painted
red, yellow, blue,
brilliant colored toys. What
essential fact did you want me to know,
that the body is the essence of spirit and so
must be in motion?

Now that I've lost my foothold, my direction, my way,
what is your message, strong spirit,
strong Grandmother,
what is the meaning of your dream-present,
a bright clock shaped like a train—
               simply that it moves?

TOMATO PIES, 25 CENTS

Tomato pies are what we called them, those days,

before Pizza came in,

at my Grandmother's restaurant,

in Trenton New Jersey.

My grandfather is rolling meatballs

in the back. He studied to be a priest in Sicily but

saved his sister Maggie from marrying a bad guy

by coming to America.

Uncle Joey is rolling dough and spooning sauce.

Uncle Joey, is always scrubbed clean,

sobered up, in a white starched shirt, after

cops delivered him home just hours before.

The waitresses are helping

themselves to handfuls of cash out of the drawer,

playing the numbers with Moon Mullins

and Shad, sent in from Broad Street. 1942,

tomato pies with cheese, 25 cents.

With anchovies, large, 50 cents.

A whole dinner is 60 cents (before 6pm).

How the soldiers, bussed in from Fort Dix,

would stand outside all the way down Warren Street,

waiting for this new taste treat,

young guys in uniform,

lined up and laughing, learning Italian,

before being shipped out to fight the last great war.

SENIOR PROM

Life can only be understood backwards,
but it must be lived forwards. . .
                          Kierkegaard

Before the return of innocence at the end,
Before I asked how can I go on without you,
Before everything cost more than thee dollars,
Before my recipe for dilled carrots,
Before I bought them Easter dresses
                but kept dreaming I forgot
Before running laps around the dining room table,
Before saying where does everything go,
Before a crystal of feeling broke open
                which will not close,
Before my children came spilling out from a wound
                which will not heal,
Before I found I was the past,
Before the long disease set in,
Before my dead grandfather appeared 40 years later
                pale and white to give me life,

One night I wore a gown of blue and white
                in layers and layers
                pale blue under pure white,

Before I let go of it all to the sky,
Before I'd say I'm afraid of eternity without you,
Before the waters were rebuked
                and we were calm,

Before the earth replenished
		with warm rain,
Before being torn between wanting to change
		and not wanting to hurt you,
Before the spiritual hydraulic lifted me from danger,
Before my left eye, left breast, left ankle broke off,
Before my heart was left beating on the sidewalk,
Before I disappointed everyone I ever knew,
Before I tried to make everyone in the world happy,

We danced the slow dance together with
		"Good Night Sweetheart"
		coming from the speakers
and time and fevers do not burn this away.

TRENTON TRANSIT

"If you go back in time, be careful,
you may stay there"

Leaving State and Broad, the bus turns left. How many times have I
been there without the fare. But this time I'm with my father.

We move down Willow to Prospect, I tell him about the box of beads,
        my
necklaces. The purple ones I lift to show how, if you love your work,
they'll sparkle. His face separates red with pain, explaining that he's
        sorry he
favors my sister's work and always will. He can't help it. The edge of my
        mind
is honed to take this, over the years, thin as steel, bends to shape,
        accommodate.

The bus is now on Prospect. I love this part. Porches narrow and sweet
        with light.
Painted like Autumn sun on wood. In two more stops we'll be there.

Past Mr. Sprague's Hardware Store, I turn a page in my book – a long
        story of a Japanese
girl who's been my friend throughout, her sly shyness teaching me
        silence. How strange to
change a living adventure by closing this book.

Gregory School on the left, now gone. Ellsworth Avenue coming up. It's
        wonderful to be with someone I've known as long as my
father. Yet I never can
        guess which of us will get off first.

In the film about the bus, the man who's whistling is not really making
      music. Behind
The screen someone else makes the sound and then it fits together
      perfectly. Not like us.

Movement inside motion on the bus is louder now. Driver will call out a
      street but it's
hardly the one we'd have chosen. How to know which is ours? If given
      a fair chance,
back then, even if we recognized the destination, we wouldn't have
      known what to name it.

ANGELO

If I were to ask what you'd like, it might be to say something kind about you,
Mention something from the past remembered with love.
And so I do. Spaghetti sauce on the bus!
You getting up at dawn to cook it, I carrying a pot
Across two states to Princeton, New Jersey
Where my professor lived
And where
Students met to read their poems
Eating the sweet red specialty
Lugged up and down stairs under a huge lid.
No one could buy that kind of cooking, at least in those days,
Although now of course
There's a restaurant on every corner
I don't know how I asked you, father, to prepare this dish
Or whether in fact you offered it knowing
Your meal was rare in American houses.
You remained at home that day while I entertained.
I think you hoped to hear them say how sensitive you were,
A loving father, and so they did, admire you this night, poets
Heard by candlelight, a fireplace, a stove.
In a different room far away, you most likely wished I'd say
They liked it, Italian food, something different for me to share. Perhaps
I would say good of you. I'll bet you went to bed easily: *this time I've made her happy.*

STAGE MAKEUP

It is where you may not want to go.

It's not what you had in mind,

imagination within hope,

but what will you do with it,

so uncertain the terrain,

the outline of music, with sounds

you have to provide yourself.

My father took me there, to *Pigliacci*,

the frightening intimacy, the veil

lifting, the feeling of gladness

or the foul mood, which? Shaking

the land inside us. We went together,

as if we needed to deepen our silence,

as if I could count hats when I got bored,

only ten years old, waiting for it to end,

but music he couldn't guard me against,

sweeping away our differences,

half a century saved in memory.

He took me to the opera, in the

War Memorial Building, downtown
Trenton. He took me to the opera
about a clown. He chose the one he
thought I'd like.

MODERATION

One cigarette a day

is all my father smoked,

no more, no less, and a

single martini taken

before his dinner. You might

say he was the very soul of

moderation.

At eighty, he swallowed

nitroglycerine pills

not to trouble anyone,

first driving to the hospital

to park his car in the lot

happy that his papers were

lined in order at home, no

inconvenience to family or

neighbors, no stepping over

the body.

I feel that last moment

as a loud sound written

beneath his life,

a bright spectacular moment

somewhat like a whistle,

his heart sounding like a

whistle, blasting high and clear,

a ship just docking from Italy

or a train

at the crossing

where he held my sister's hand

on her way to music lessons,

looking back at me on the porch

in the silence before the whistle.

NETTIE

How to make it up to her?
  She was no

stronger than the wheat
  her father carried

to the altar in Sicily for his penance,
  she was that frail, like the

pale yellow Italian sun . . .
  others becoming animals as

they grew but she. . . she
  turning into the sky and

the ocean until
  there was finally no place

else she could go.
  I would make her broth

if the dead could drink, bring it in a tin cup.
  I would take the stories out of the

Vial of breath I've saved
  in case my own breath should stop.

I'd give it to her, if it would help, but
  this is of no use to her now.

I have so little to give up,
  except—maybe, fear—which

exists only for itself.
  Out of the crescent moon,

from these shapes
  I hear my father's voice

calling me again, last night, low and
  filled with a holding heart.

I'd never heard before. *Come
  to yourself*, he said.

In all her needs and through
  meanings of her crying

the only thing left
  is my father's voice

stronger than memory.
  That was always my trouble

in trying to save her, his voice.
  Now I remember her grief,

how she stood by my father's
  chair as he stared angrily

out the window. There she is,
  so slim. She wears a long

silken dress, her hands are like first speech.
   This is progress I think, her sitting still

for it without falling apart—
   he, finally speaking to me.

The dead are just as
   involved as anyone else if you listen closely.

The are here to work it out with the living.

JUDY AND ME

From time to time

someone would ask

how many children were

in our family.

It was always the same,

I'd snap (ready) "just

one – me – and a broken

umbrella handle."

My father always laughed

at that entangled wit,

hardly funny now

it seems, my sister as

an object.

Did description amuse him?

Or the use of skewed language?

What did it mean?

What did it say?

Why such a thought?

How is it

my father smiled at

the idea of a handle

so crippled?

What if the umbrella

could have opened?

SUMMER IN THE CONVENT

As a child, spending my days, I thought I'd amuse

them with my mother's favorite story

about the pretentious lady who had a butler

who answered the door in his fancy way.

One day the rabbit came to deliver the lawn

fertilizer, asking to see the lady in charge.

Mrs. TurTELL is down by the well,

came the haughty reply. Then an icy answer:

Tell her Mr. RabBIT is Here With The Shit.

The nuns moved noiselessly away to their own

gardens except in the coloring book of my memory.

I only wanted to make them happy.

TO HIS HOUSE

I liked the parties best,

where my parents' friends

came late at night,

men around the table

playing cards,

women on the sofa, talking –

highballs for everyone,

cold cuts on a platter.

But something always ruined it

settling like stale smoke

when the jokes were gone.

Mr. Brettell

in his white silk shirt

saying, "I'll give it to you

right off my back" – then

to hoots and hollers,

doing just that, taking it off –

right there – to give to my sister.

The sorry part was when I said

"How about me?"

and him telling me to come

by his house tomorrow

and I'd get one too.

By that time the party

was over.

And with what feelings

did I walk two blocks

to knock on his door,

and with what thoughts

did he stand there,

opening, barely opening,

just enough to shove a shirt

rolled tight like a ball

into my arms.

REPLACING LOSS

For Jan

When our mothers

were children together,

they never knew

you'd wait for me

to be born,

and so you did, when

you were three months

old, I was born to be your

friend, and live just

down the street,

where we played,

and spent a life with dolls,

two little girls

in their backyards,

among the flowers

with their gowns,

until the place

was only in our thoughts

and even then we stayed

returning

in our minds to talk.

This all vanished suddenly

last Fall,

taking Japonica trees,

the Virgin Mary's statue,

talcum jars filled with

Queen Anne's lace,

library books on

varnished chairs,

hot baloney sandwiches

and schoolyard stairs,

where you waited,

as you do now,

after a silent Winter,

resuming a lifelong

conversation,

which goes on.

THINGS THAT HURRIED BY

Once I was lighting a fire

for my sister and the head

of the match snapped off,

popping in my eye.

She looked at me with such concern

Her mouth crinkled at the corners

with fear and love

I'd never seen.

It seems I could live

with one eye after that.

I thought I could

spend my time doing

small tasks like polishing

a crystal bowl with a soft cloth,

its cut glass sides

edged by fear and light.

Once I told my father that he

didn't take my work

seriously

and his brown eyes filled with

a look I'd never seen

something protective

like mist then something worse,

naked in the rain,

like the word *seriously*.

I take that to bed with me,

wrapping myself in it

like a sweater made in

Yugoslavia or Bulgaria,

a look rough as wool,

wishing I were in Italy

where it wasn't so cold.

Once my mother said to return

Kathy's call so she'd know

the message was received.

I screamed that I would call

when I wanted.

I'd never raised my voice

to my mother

as she had never

raised hers to me.

She hurried past

to her bedroom without looking up.

She didn't look up.

MARKINGS

For my sister Judy (1930-1984)

Although the house appears close at hand

There is a cliff between us

Covered with ice

           therefore the only

Route is the long way 'round.

In the house are country people

Visiting on a Saturday night

With new permed hair and

Comfortable dresses.

Who wouldn't like to be among them,

On a simple couch talking

Together, in a slightly formal way, sitting

           carefully upon our chairs

Yet we must drive through long

Roads among towns and surrounding

Villages to get there and once arrived,

Endure the long way back.

There is no excitement in the house,

No music, no refreshments. But

These are the people who have made their peace,

And after our short time together,

We lose our way in the dark, returning home.

These are the people we wanted to be with

               for an evening

Before their spin to eternity.

This is the night, when later we speak

About loss

               will be the night we have lost.

THIS IS

The September of our Loss

The old man who is to die
Takes a nap anyway.

I admire that.

YOU COULD NOT SAY
SHE WAS OF THIS EARTH

for Nettie Zoda Cavalieri (1903-1956)

If milk curdled she said the fairies did it.

If her face itched

she believed it was brushed by a saint.

Lovely, more than anything else.

she rose from the cathedral of childhood

vivid in the fields

while the world turned to rust and wheels.

She thought there was love

in objects and with her faith

said "Thank you frying pan.

Thank you table." This would be twenty years

before I'd be born

And she would be my mother who still comes to me

During a certain vibration of song

which I play furtively so no one else can hear.

MEETING OF THE HEAVENLY ANCESTORS

They love a spectacle so I wear
a light airy dress,
it is fitting attire
to be in their midst,
yet I feel naked moving
so lightly under my gown,
I hear voices
through the rain
saying nothing of the self is here
but what will yet be written,
they introduce me to the woman
who will be my mother
saying she is so virtuous
she does not have to do good deeds,
she is a supreme animal on earth,
unlike other creatures
who must wash what they find
in order to eat.

PALACE OF LISTENING

I called on my mother
in the night
tugging her name
like a testament
and she appeared
through the face of a man
sitting on a doorstep

To let me know
I'd made contact
she turned her head
toward the light
so I could see the
tears in her eyes.

THE MAGICIAN

I wish I could say
he was always with us
among the dark furniture
of childhood, keeping our mild chances and
half-hearted dreams from thinning,

One could count on him,
strange as Venus, to
appear at odd places
declaring immortality
when least expected,

Once I knew him well
in the garden. He told
the shocking truth
that the present
has nothing to do with the past,

As you might expect
the force of this made
the cat jump from the hedge,

The sliver of his voice
is in our ears
making the world over
without envy,

When we were little girls
—between the lilies

and the bridal wreath—
loving dolls was our industry
and we worked as hard
as immigrants at it,
making plates of grass
and rooms of leaves,

He was there sweetening
the day with its clock of milk
as he is now, combining
the right amount of whites
and greens, virtue and remembrance.

IN SEARCH OF MY GRANDFATHER — Three Sestinas

1. *In Search of my Grandfather*: Rome

The first thing you notice is the flight attendant
stealing a crying child's nose,
like my grandfather, who couldn't speak English,
communicating love to me.
Yeats said the center does not hold
yet time forms a center in the hills north of Rome.

The air is drenched with my father's life in Rome
with the wine of the Tiber attendant
to the walls of this old city which hold
memories of places I've never been; the nose
of a fountain called Triton, finds me
leaning in with others throwing coins and English

Prayers to Arena, Rome's goddess, chanting the English
words "The reverse of amore is Rome."
Saint Assisi protects all this, the city and me.
Garibaldi united Italy making Rome attendant
to its states, as leader, putting its nose
out into the world, grabbing all the power it could hold.

The creation of the heavens and the earth hold
the universe of Adam and Eve while our English
eyes search the Sistine for the nose
of a serpent creeping across the seven hills of Rome.

How can I find what is gone here, the past attendant,
to the blood of my ancestors still lost on me.

The pines of the surrounding land speak to me
telling of roads toward Tuscany which hold
the secrets of the past, a man who lived attendant
to a world of wealth in Florence, who left for English
soil and a poverty unknown. I think of this in Rome
as we leave to find Siena and Padua. I follow my nose

From city to city as our cars nose
through countrysides and hills which call me
on, past abandoned farms, tile roofs, pink walls, Rome.
Goodbye, Grandfather whose memory I hold,
Goodbye, Rafael, you saw this city last, before English
grief reframed your life with all its pain attendant.

As the fog lifts over the mountains of Bologna, attendant
to the yellow salmon brown pink of Italy, an English
thought reminds us that the center we seek will not hold.

2. *In Search of my Grandfather*: Florence

When you were in Siena what did you see
on these crooked streets where no one knew you,
where you studied during undergraduate days.
My dreams of this are in a cup which fills to spill
its sides with feelings which have no language,
and must be found, along with clean paper to write this.

Cats have no memory, yet they recognize. This
thought is with me because I came to Siena to see

what I would recognize. You walked with the language
of these Italian birds flying by, as flew near you
years before the religious war would spill
inside your heart and lead you away from Italy's quiet days.

Florence was where you stayed and had your bride during days
numbered in their joy — Firenze — sweet capital of this
country before it moved to Rome. Floods still spill
these shores every hundred years. One can see
grief behind an old city inside old walls you
walked, a cemetery of hopes buried in your language.

Michelangelo began statues, imprisoned in a language
of stone, commissioned by Julius those days
then called back to Rome. Did you
also leave undone figures in your memory, as this
marble block holds something for us to see –
unfinished shapes and suggestions which spill

To our imaginations for completion, which spill
from the prison of marble to the freedom of language.
Famous David is 500 years old and we see
a figure you looked at 100 years ago during your days
here. We both stood nearby a perfect form, studying this
large right hand which denotes strength. Did you

Stand like this and walk closer? How could you
know I would be here so long after you, ready to spill
my thoughts on paper, taking all this
as my own, the city of flowers in sunlight, the language
of Florence in the rain, the pain of Dante during the days
where Latin was transformed to sounds we'd say and see.

The marble quarried in this region as language
left standing. The white, red, and green from early days
stays, and what the young man Rafael saw, I now see.

3. *In Search of my Grandfather*: Venice

Two different climates meet near Padua. From the sea
a warmth, from the Apennines, the Austrian cold.
This moves us nearer Venice past the apple trees
pinned against their wires, the pruned grape vine
ready to burst, the plastic over its seedling ground,
the peace of mountains north of Padua, past the flat

Land we travel so we can reach Venezia. The villas are flat
wide houses where Italians fought Germans until the sea
of Venice added mercy to the misery of this bloody ground.
Once, Venetian horse traders and fishermen worked their cold
wind and waters to win ten centuries of power, the vine
of time runs through this country's broken trees.

It is strange to say in Venice that there are now no trees
but that 450 bridges cross centuries of water winding flat
within its alleys. Here the canals weave a vine
within a golden city sinking wooden pilings to a sea
of time. My father left in 1912 and his cold
childhood still floats through the silt of sinking ground.

The first shipyard in all the world existed on this ground.
I love the thought of Venice emerging from the trees
of 13th century beliefs to venture into the earth's cold
waters. Marco Polo crossed a map people thought was flat,
to pick the flowers and the spices of the world by sea
tossing across the oceans a city's green imperial vine.

My Venetian father never lost his regal past, the vine
of glory in his spine. He knew his early ground
was that of palaces and kings, and then the strange sea
of love changed his plans and drew him deep inside the trees
of Sicily to find a bride so unlike him that the flat
northern air would make the lemon trees die of cold.

Through the wide open windows of Sicily the cold air
seldom enters. Only the winds breathe. Only the vine
of Aetna's smoke moves up the coast to praise its flat
lands above a river of lava rising from ancient ground.
Since Norman times grain grew beyond these trees
and is brought to altars, wheat of lava and the sea.

We speed faster than the sun travels toward the sea.
It seems our lives are racing past these olive trees
hungry to grow our heart's slow root in Italy's ground.

EXPRESSION

Where is the little girl?
   sitting on the steps

What is she doing?
   holding a cardboard box

It stands on end. It has
   a tiny golden clasp which can open.

Inside there are small blue hangers
   holding dolls' clothes.

Two drawers beneath pull out.
   She pulls them and looks inside –

Mysterious pieces of fabric
   dark red velvet, cream satin squares

blue lace. She stares

for minutes and minutes of pleasure,
   folding, smoothing, touching.

Where does she go?
   she stands and walks into the house.

This is the same house she'll dream
   twenty years later is empty, where

No one is home, where
    there is dark in every room

And no matter who she calls,
    no one will answer.

What does she feel?
    something that has no name.

She will sleep in the silence
    of that moment – alone on the steps

Walking into the empty house
    seeing there is no mother, father sister

maybe there never was.

Later the doll's clothes become
    real clothes. There will be real dolls.

She will fold soft blankets,
    sweet wool, small bonnets, knit booties

pink dresses into cool dark drawers.

BLUE-GREEN SPIRIT

Oh Dream Wanderer

with your message stick

with your rooster crowing,

Where is the voice I spoke

after I was dead

before I was born?

How much has been left by the wayside?

If every dream were a tattoo

how would I look?

Would I start loving my skin

turning in the light

holding up my arm to understand

what each flower means?

They say because the female bird

can't sing

she flies only during Summer in Sweden,

Oh no, listen,

she is connected to the divine and

sings of her taste for life and death,

She sings until heard,

it is the voice we share where

nothing is lost.

ABOUT THE AUTHOR

GRACE CAVALIERI is the author of sixteen books and chapbooks of poetry, including *Water on the Sun*, (*Acqua sul sole*), Bordighera Prize winner 2006, translated to Italian by Maria Enrico. More recently she published: *Gotta Go Now* (2012), *Millie's Sunshine Tiki Villas* (2011), and *Sounds Like Something I Would Say* (2010) from Casa Menendez Press. She has also written texts and lyrics performed for opera, television and film. Her newest publication is an Italian translation of *What I Would Do For Love:* Poems in the Voice of Mary Wollstonecraft, 1759-1797. titled, *Cosa Farei Per Amore,* translated by Sabine Pascarelli (2013). Cavalieri's awards include the Pen-Fiction Award, the Allen Ginsberg Poetry Awards (1993 & 2013), a Paterson Prize, the National Commission on Working Women, the American Association of University Women, the in-augural Folger Columbia Award for "significant contributions to poetry;" plus AWP's 2013 "George Garret Award" for "Service to Literature." She's the featured poetry columnist for *The Washington Independent Review of Books.* She founded and still produces "The Poet and the Poem" for public radio, celebrating thirty-seven years on-air, now recorded at The Library of Congress, awarded The Silver Medal by The Corporation for Public Broadcasting. She serves on the national advisory board of the American Initiative For Italian Culture.

VIA FOLIOS
A refereed book series dedicated to the culture of Italians and Italian Americans.

MARISA FRASCA. *Via incanto* Vol 96 Poetry. $11

DOUG GLADSTONE. *Carving a Niche for Himself* Vol 95 History. $12

MARIA TERRONE. *Eye to Eye* Vol 94 Poetry. $15

CONSTANCE SANCETTA. *Here in Cerchio* Vol 93 Local History. $15

MARIA MAZZIOTTI GILLAN. *Ancestors' Song* Vol 92 Poetry. $14

DARRELL FUSARO. *What if Godzilla Just Wanted a Hug?* Vol ? Essays. $TBA

MICHAEL PARENTI. *Waiting for Yesterday: Pages from a Street Kid's Life.* Vol 90 Memoir. $15

ANNIE LANZILOTTO, *Schistsong*, Vol. 89. Poetry, $15

EMANUEL DI PASQUALE, *Love Lines*, Vol. 88. Poetry, $10

CAROSONE & LOGIUDICE. *Our Naked Lives.* Vol 87 Essays. $15

JAMES PERICONI. *Strangers in a Strange Land: A Survey of Italian-Language American Books.* Vol. 86. Book History. $24

DANIELA GIOSEFFI, *Escaping La Vita Della Cucina*, Vol. 85. Essays & Creative Writing. $22

MARIA FAMÀ, *Mystics in the Family*, Vol. 84. Poetry, $10

ROSSANA DEL ZIO, *From Bread and Tomatoes to Zuppa di Pesce "Ciambotto"*, Vol. 83. $15

LORENZO DELBOCA, *Polentoni*, Vol. 82. Italian Studies, $15

SAMUEL GHELLI, *A Reference Grammar*, Vol. 81. Italian Language. $36

ROSS TALARICO, *Sled Run*, Vol. 80. Fiction. $15

FRED MISURELLA, *Only Sons*, Vol. 79. Fiction. $14

FRANK LENTRICCHIA, *The Portable Lentricchia*, Vol. 78. Fiction. $16

RICHARD VETERE, *The Other Colors in a Snow Storm*, Vol. 77. Poetry. $10

GARIBALDI LAPOLLA, *Fire in the Flesh*, Vol. 76 Fiction & Criticism. $25

GEORGE GUIDA, *The Pope Stories*, Vol. 75 Prose. $15

ROBERT VISCUSI, *Ellis Island*, Vol. 74. Poetry. $28

ELENA GIANINI BELOTTI, *The Bitter Taste of Strangers Bread*, Vol. 73, Fiction, $24

PINO APRILE, *Terroni*, Vol. 72, Italian Studies, $20

EMANUEL DI PASQUALE, *Harvest*, Vol. 71, Poetry, $10

ROBERT ZWEIG, *Return to Naples*, Vol. 70, Memoir, $16

AIROS & CAPPELLI, *Guido*, Vol. 69, Italian/American Studies, $12

FRED GARDAPHÉ, *Moustache Pete is Dead! Long Live Moustache Pete!*, Vol. 67, Literature/Oral History, $12

PAOLO RUFFILLI, *Dark Room/Camera oscura*, Vol. 66, Poetry, $11

HELEN BAROLINI, *Crossing the Alps*, Vol. 65, Fiction, $14

COSMO FERRARA, *Profiles of Italian Americans*, Vol. 64, Italian Americana, $16

GIL FAGIANI, *Chianti in Connecticut*, Vol. 63, Poetry, $10

BASSETTI & D'ACQUINO, *Italic Lessons*, Vol. 62, Italian/American Studies, $10

CAVALIERI & PASCARELLI, Eds., *The Poet's Cookbook*, Vol. 61, Poetry/Recipes, $12

EMANUEL DI PASQUALE, *Siciliana*, Vol. 60, Poetry, $8

NATALIA COSTA, Ed., *Bufalini*, Vol. 59, Poetry. $18.

RICHARD VETERE, *Baroque*, Vol. 58, Fiction. $18.

LEWIS TURCO, *La Famiglia/The Family*, Vol. 57, Memoir, $15

NICK JAMES MILETI, *The Unscrupulous*, Vol. 56, Humanities, $20

BASSETTI, ACCOLLA, D'AQUINO, *Italici: An Encounter with Piero Bassetti*, Vol. 55, Italian Studies, $8

Bordighera Press is an imprint of Bordighera, Incorporated, an independently owned not-for-profit scholarly organization that has no legal affiliation with the University of Central Florida or with The John D. Calandra Italian American Institute, Queens College/CUNY.

GIOSE RIMANELLI, *The Three-legged One*, Vol. 54, Fiction, $15

CHARLES KLOPP, *Bele Antiche Stòrie*, Vol. 53, Criticism, $25

JOSEPH RICAPITO, *Second Wave*, Vol. 52, Poetry, $12

GARY MORMINO, *Italians in Florida*, Vol. 51, History, $15

GIANFRANCO ANGELUCCI, *Federico F.*, Vol. 50, Fiction, $15

ANTHONY VALERIO, *The Little Sailor*, Vol. 49, Memoir, $9

ROSS TALARICO, *The Reptilian Interludes*, Vol. 48, Poetry, $15

RACHEL GUIDO DE VRIES, *Teeny Tiny Tino's Fishing Story*, Vol. 47, Children's Literature, $6

EMANUEL DI PASQUALE, *Writing Anew*, Vol. 46, Poetry, $15

MARIA FAMÀ, *Looking For Cover*, Vol. 45, Poetry, $12

ANTHONY VALERIO, *Toni Cade Bambara's One Sicilian Night*, Vol. 44, Poetry, $10

EMANUEL CARNEVALI, Dennis Barone, Ed., *Furnished Rooms*, Vol. 43, Poetry, $14

BRENT ADKINS, et al., Ed., *Shifting Borders, Negotiating Places*, Vol. 42, Proceedings, $18

GEORGE GUIDA, *Low Italian*, Vol. 41, Poetry, $11

GARDAPHÈ, GIORDANO, TAMBURRI, *Introducing Italian Americana*, Vol. 40, Italian/American Studies, $10

DANIELA GIOSEFFI, *Blood Autumn/Autunno di sangue*, Vol. 39, Poetry, $15/$25

FRED MISURELLA, *Lies to Live by*, Vol. 38, Stories, $15

STEVEN BELLUSCIO, *Constructing a Bibliography*, Vol. 37, Italian Americana, $15

ANTHONY JULIAN TAMBURRI, Ed., *Italian Cultural Studies 2002*, Vol. 36, Essays, $18

BEA TUSIANI, *con amore*, Vol. 35, Memoir, $19

FLAVIA BRIZIO-SKOV, Ed., *Reconstructing Societies in the Aftermath of War*, Vol. 34, History, $30

TAMBURRI, et al., Eds., *Italian Cultural Studies 2001*, Vol. 33, Essays, $18

ELIZABETH G. MESSINA, Ed., *In Our Own Voices*, Vol. 32, Italian/American Studies, $25

STANISLAO G. PUGLIESE, *Desperate Inscriptions*, Vol. 31, History, $12

HOSTERT & TAMBURRI, Eds., *Screening Ethnicity*, Vol. 30, Italian/American Culture, $25

G. PARATI & B. LAWTON, Eds., *Italian Cultural Studies*, Vol. 29, Essays, $18

HELEN BAROLINI, *More Italian Hours*, Vol. 28, Fiction, $16

FRANCO NASI, Ed., *Intorno alla Via Emilia*, Vol. 27, Culture, $16

ARTHUR L. CLEMENTS, *The Book of Madness & Love*, Vol. 26, Poetry, $10

JOHN CASEY, et al., *Imagining Humanity*, Vol. 25, Interdisciplinary Studies, $18

ROBERT LIMA, *Sardinia/Sardegna*, Vol. 24, Poetry, $10

DANIELA GIOSEFFI, *Going On*, Vol. 23, Poetry, $10

ROSS TALARICO, *The Journey Home*, Vol. 22, Poetry, $12

EMANUEL DI PASQUALE, *The Silver Lake Love Poems*, Vol. 21, Poetry, $7

JOSEPH TUSIANI, *Ethnicity*, Vol. 20, Poetry, $12

JENNIFER LAGIER, *Second Class Citizen*, Vol. 19, Poetry, $8

FELIX STEFANILE, *The Country of Absence*, Vol. 18, Poetry, $9

PHILIP CANNISTRARO, *Blackshirts*, Vol. 17, History, $12

LUIGI RUSTICHELLI, Ed., *Seminario sul racconto*, Vol. 16, Narrative, $10

LEWIS TURCO, *Shaking the Family Tree*, Vol. 15, Memoirs, $9

LUIGI RUSTICHELLI, Ed., *Seminario sulla drammaturgia*, Vol. 14, Theater/Essays, $10

FRED GARDAPHÈ, *Moustache Pete is Dead! Long Live Moustache Pete!*, Vol. 13, Oral Literature, $10

JONE GAILLARD CORSI, *Il libretto d'autore*, 1860–1930, Vol. 12, Criticism, $17

HELEN BAROLINI, *Chiaroscuro: Essays of Identity*, Vol. 11, Essays, $15

PICARAZZI & FEINSTEIN, Eds., *An African Harlequin in Milan*, Vol. 10, Theater/Essays, $15

JOSEPH RICAPITO, *Florentine Streets & Other Poems*, Vol. 9, Poetry, $9

FRED MISURELLA, *Short Time*, Vol. 8, Novella, $7

NED CONDINI, *Quartettsatz*, Vol. 7, Poetry, $7

ANTHONY JULIAN TAMBURRI, Ed. *Fuori: Essays by Italian/American Lesbians and Gays*, Vol. 6, Essays, $10

ANTONIO GRAMSCI, P. Verdicchio, Trans. & Intro. , *The Southern Question*, Vol. 5, Social Criticism, $5

DANIELA GIOSEFFI, *Word Wounds & Water Flowers*, Vol. 4, Poetry, $8

WILEY FEINSTEIN, *Humility's Deceit: Calvino Reading Ariosto Reading Calvino*, Vol. 3, Criticism, $10

PAOLO A. GIORDANO, Ed., *Joseph Tusiani: Poet, Translator, Humanist*, Vol. 2, Criticism, $25

ROBERT VISCUSI, *Oration Upon the Most Recent Death of Christopher Columbus*, Vol. 1, Poetry, $3

CPSIA information can be obtained at www.ICGtesting.com
Printed in the USA
LVOW07s2014101215

466280LV00009B/1128/P